The Scientist's Apprentice

Written by Brandon Robshaw

Illustrated by Lala Stellune

Collins

Chapter 1

The first time Marcus Morris saw Professor Digory Kranium, he was up a tree. The professor was up the tree, that is. Marcus was in his garden sitting in a deckchair and enjoying his library book about dinosaurs. He was reading about the size of the Tyrannosaurus Rex's teeth (they grew up to 30 centimetres) when he heard a rustling and bustling. It was coming from the cherry tree in the next-door garden. Marcus looked over the hedge and saw a man in a tweed suit and a long beard, balanced on a branch. He was peering at something through a magnifying glass.

3

The man was muttering, "15, 16, 17 ... Oh, keep still, will you ... Start again ... One, two, three ... oh, dear, no, don't – !"

A small red insect rose from the branch and flew away. The man in the tree grabbed at it, dropped his magnifying glass and overbalanced. He fell, landing in a lavender bush on Marcus's side of the hedge.

The man got up, brushing leaves and twigs
off his suit. He caught sight of Marcus and said,
"Do excuse me, I seem to have arrived in your garden."

"That's all right," Marcus said.

"I'm your new neighbour. Professor Digory Kranium."

Marcus had seen
the removal van yesterday.
He'd been extremely curious
about it. The removals
workers had unloaded lots
of crates with foreign writing
on, as well as some strange,
complicated machinery
and a massive telescope.

"Pleased to meet you,"
Marcus said politely.
"I'm Marcus. Er ... what
were you doing up there?"

"Pursuing a ladybird,"
the professor replied.
"I thought it had 25 spots,
you see. Remarkable.
That would be a UK record!
Not my main area
of research, you
understand, but–"

"Are you a scientist?"

7

"Smart boy!" said the professor. "And I must get back to work. Do you think I might come through your house? It'd save me climbing over the hedge."

"Of course!" Marcus put down his book and led the professor through the back door. His mum and dad were drinking coffee in the kitchen. They looked up in surprise.

"This is Professor Kranium!" said Marcus. "He lives next door and he's a scientist!"

"Oh, we know the professor!" said Marcus's dad. "He gives talks at my school." (Marcus's dad was a teacher.) "In fact, it was me who told him the house next door was for sale."

"Would you care for a coffee, professor?" asked Marcus's mum.

The professor shook his head. "Better get back to work, I'm afraid. I have a most interesting project in hand. Speaking of which ..." He looked at Marcus. "I need an assistant. An apprentice, if you will. I wonder if your son might care to help, for a little pocket money?"

Marcus's mum looked doubtful. "He's quite busy with his schoolwork."

"It would only be at weekends," said the professor.

"And I'd learn lots about science, Mum!" said Marcus.

"Not sure he'd be a very good apprentice," said Marcus's dad. "He's terribly scatty."

"He seems like a smart boy to me," said the professor. "He reads books about dinosaurs in his spare time!"

"Please, Dad? Mum? Please …?"

Chapter 2

Marcus was so pleased that his mum and dad had agreed, especially when he saw the professor's laboratory. There were shelves with bottles of chemicals, all different colours like jars in a sweetshop. There was a workbench with Bunsen burners. A computer with an animated screensaver of a snake chasing its own tail. An electronic whiteboard covered in complicated maths equations. A skeleton on a stand in one corner. And there was a contraption that looked like a photo booth – it had two chairs facing each other, and lots of buttons, dials and flashing lights at the side. A black cat with green eyes sat on one of the seats. The other was empty.

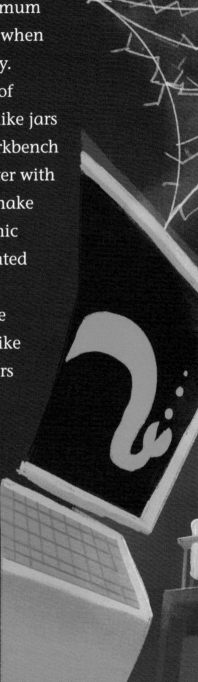

"That," said the professor proudly, "is my Autosomatic Transpositioner!"

"Your *what?*" asked Marcus.

"To put it in plain language," said the professor, "it's a body-swap machine."

"A body-swap machine? You mean …?"

"Or a mind-swap machine," said the professor. "Whichever you prefer."

"You can put a person's mind in another body?" Marcus wondered whether Professor Kranium was joking. Yet he seemed perfectly serious.

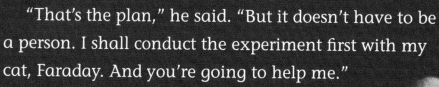

"That's the plan," he said. "But it doesn't have to be a person. I shall conduct the experiment first with my cat, Faraday. And you're going to help me."

"You want me to swap minds with the cat?" asked Marcus.

"I wouldn't ask you to do that, Marcus! *I* shall swap. All you have to do is press this button here." The professor pointed to a glowing red button. "If all goes to plan, Faraday and I will swap bodies. And then I'll need you to press the button again to swap us back." He chuckled. "I wouldn't want to be a cat for the rest of my life!"

"Well, OK–" Marcus began, but just then there was a knock at the door.

"That'll be the plutonium I ordered.
For another experiment. Wait there and don't
touch anything!" The professor rushed from the room.

Marcus stared at the machine. He felt curious about
what it would feel like inside. The professor had told
him not to touch anything, but surely sitting down
wouldn't count? He went inside and sat on the chair
opposite the cat.

The cat stared at Marcus. It was weird to think that in a few moments that would be the professor. Marcus wondered if he'd let him have a turn afterwards. It would be fun to try life as a cat for a while …

A small brown moth came fluttering into the body swap machine.

Chapter 3

The moth flew between Marcus and Faraday.

This seemed to annoy the cat. Faraday swiped at the moth with its paw and missed. The moth danced around just out of reach.

The cat jumped and swiped again.

Faraday's paw hit the red button – just as the moth flew in front of Marcus's face.

For a second, Marcus saw the moth's little black eyes staring into his. And then something very strange happened.

A beam of silver light flowed between him and the moth. Marcus felt his mind, his thoughts, somehow leaving his body and flowing along the silver beam. For a moment, everything went black.

And when he could see again, he found he was staring into *his own face.*

But his face didn't look normal. It was more like a collage, broken up into hundreds of little overlapping squares. But it was definitely him. *This is how a moth would see,* thought Marcus. *They have compound eyes.*

I have compound eyes!

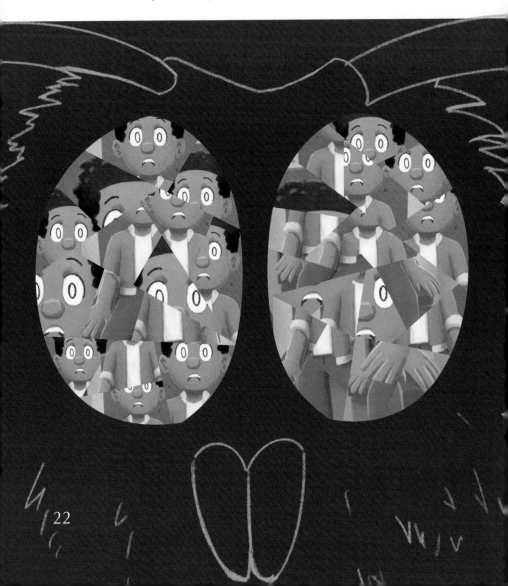

Marcus flapped his wings and rose higher. He felt lighter than air. This was great! He could have a lot of fun as a moth before the professor changed him back.

The professor came back into the room. "Got my plutonium, now, so – Marcus? Marcus? Are you all right?"

Marcus was flitting around at head height and looked down to see his normal body slumped in the body-swap machine. Its eyes were vacant, its mouth gaping open. *The moth doesn't know what's going on,* Marcus thought. *It must be a shock if you're a moth to suddenly find yourself in a human body.*

"Marcus! What's happened to you?"

Marcus tried to call out. But he couldn't speak.

Moths didn't have lungs, or voice boxes, he realised.

They can't make a sound.

I can't make a sound!

Chapter 4

"Marcus!" said the professor. "I told you not to touch anything! What have you done?"

Marcus flew in front of Professor Kranium's face, fluttering up and down to get his attention. The professor swatted him away, and Marcus had to dodge.

The professor approached moth-Marcus. It was still slumped in the machine with drool dribbling down its chin. The professor shook moth-Marcus's arm.

Moth-Marcus rose clumsily to its feet, nearly falling over. It began to stagger around in circles, flapping its arms as if trying to take off. It crashed into the French window and stopped, but its arms still flapped helplessly up and down.

The professor frowned and rubbed his beard thoughtfully, staring at Faraday. The cat was now sitting on the floor, yawning.

"Is that you, Marcus?" the professor asked. "You've swapped bodies, haven't you?"

The cat just stared back at him.

"Marcus? If you're Marcus, raise a paw!"

The cat yawned again and scratched behind its ear.

"Let's get you back in the Transpositioner," said the professor. "We can swap you back–"

Again, Marcus tried to get Professor Kranium's attention, dancing around in the air.

"Go away!" said the professor. He cupped his hands around Marcus and carried him over to the French window.

"Clear off!" He opened the window and shooed
Marcus out into the garden. Moth-Marcus tried
to follow, but the professor grabbed it by the arm.
"You're not going anywhere, Faraday!"

The French window slammed shut. Marcus found
himself out in the garden, all alone.

No, not quite alone.

A hungry-looking sparrow with beady eyes was
swooping down towards him.

Chapter 5

Marcus darted away. The sparrow's beak missed
him by a millimetre – he felt the wind of it
pass him. The rush of air was enough to send him
fluttering sideways.

I'm so small and fragile,
Marcus thought.

The sparrow rose,
wheeled around and
swooped again.
Marcus twitched his
wings and dodged.
The bird's beady
eyes seemed to blaze
with fury.

Out in the open,
the sparrow would get Marcus
sooner or later. He must hide!
He sped to the drainpipe at the side of the house and
tucked himself behind it. The sparrow couldn't reach
him there. It flew around for a bit, then gave up and
flew away in search of easier prey.

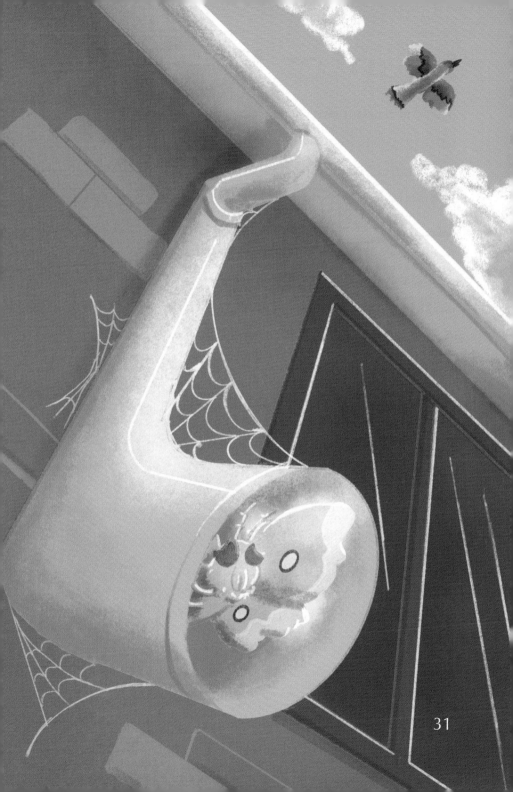

31

Phew! If moths had lungs, Marcus would have taken a deep breath. What was he going to do?

He had to get himself swapped back somehow – and fast. Moths didn't live long! Just a few weeks. If Marcus couldn't change back before then …

His parents would never know what had happened. They'd think that moth-Marcus was him – they'd have a zombie for a son! He wished he could talk to them and explain. All the times he'd been cross and argued with his parents came flooding back. *If I get out of this, I'm going to be really nice to them*, he thought. *I'll be the best son ever.*

He had to get home. Somehow he'd make his mum and dad understand.

Marcus cautiously crawled out from behind the drainpipe. He tried to take off.

Nothing happened. His wings were beating but he wasn't going anywhere. Something was sticking to him. Too late, he realised what had happened.

He had blundered into a spider's web.

The spider was creeping down the web towards him. It was a big, speckled creature with long angled legs. It appeared to be licking its lips.

This is just about the worst Saturday I've ever had, thought Marcus.

Chapter 6

Think, Marcus told himself. *You're smarter than a moth.*
A moth would just struggle blindly, and the harder it
struggled, the more stuck it would get.

Marcus stopped moving. The spider stopped too.
Now that the web was still, the spider didn't seem sure
if its prey was there.

He mustn't move his wings, Marcus realised. They were big and fragile, and if they got stuck to the web, he wouldn't stand a chance. At the moment, it was just his furry underbelly that was stuck.

Carefully, cautiously, he began to pick at the web with his legs, trying to get his body free. Yes – he could feel it pulling away. His six little feet gradually broke through the sticky strands ...

A sudden movement made the web shake again and the spider scuttled towards him.

In the nick of time, Marcus broke free, beating his wings to rise into the air.

He flew over the hedge into his own garden. There was his house, with the kitchen window open. *I want my mum,* Marcus thought. *Help me, Mum!*

He flew in through the window. His mother was working on her laptop at the table. He landed on her hand – but she shook him off with a shout of disgust. She didn't like moths, Marcus remembered.

"It's me, Mum!" he tried to shout – but of course no sound came out.

There was a knock at the door. Marcus's mum got up to answer it. Marcus flew into the hall after her.

The professor stood on the doorstep with somebody who looked very like Marcus. It didn't seem to be moth-Marcus anymore. It wasn't flapping its arms or drooling. *But it's not* me, thought Marcus – *so who is it?*

"Er, I'm afraid there's been a slight mishap with your son," the professor said. "I'm sure I can fix it but ... something rather strange has occurred."

The person who looked like Marcus opened its mouth. "Miaow," it said.

At once Marcus understood what had happened. The professor had swapped Faraday and moth-Marcus. So now the moth was in the cat's body and the cat was in Marcus's body!

Chapter 7

"Is this some kind of joke?" said Marcus's mum.

"Miaow!" said cat-Marcus.

"Let's go and sit down," the professor said. "I'll try to explain ..."

They went into the kitchen. Cat-Marcus immediately sat down by the fridge and looked at it hopefully.

"Marcus – what are you doing?" asked his mum.

"Miaow?"

"The thing is, you see – " the professor began.

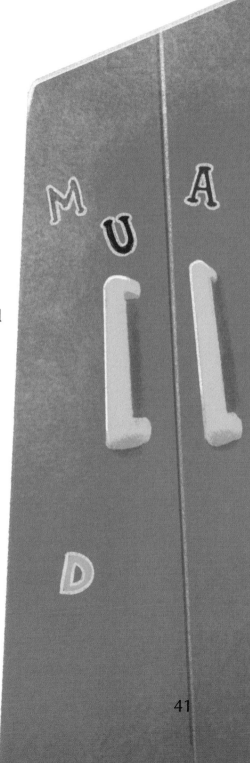

Desperately, Marcus swooped in front of them.

"What's that horrible insect doing?" said Marcus's mum. "Shoo!"

How could Marcus communicate? He couldn't handle a pen. There were magnetic letters on the fridge, but they'd be too heavy to lift.

Suddenly, Marcus's mind went into top gear! He flew over to his mum's laptop.

The professor went to swat him away, but Marcus managed to land on the *i* key. Then the *a*. Then the *m*. Then another *m* ...

"The moth's spelling something out!" said the professor excitedly. "Iammarcus ... I am Marcus!"

"What?" said Marcus's mother. "You're Marcus? What do you mean?"

"I mean I can sort this out, thank goodness!" The professor scooped up Marcus in one hand and with the other took cat-Marcus's arm. "We'll be right back!"

It didn't take long for the body-swap machine to do its job. Minutes later, Marcus was back in his body, and the moth and the cat were back in theirs.

"I hope you've learnt your lesson," said the professor sternly. "I asked you not to touch anything."

Marcus was so happy to be himself again. Faraday seemed glad, too. He was eating from a bowl of food. The moth had flitted into the garden. Marcus hoped it could avoid sparrows and spiders.

"I only sat on the seat!" Marcus said. "It was Faraday who pressed the button. Still – at least we know it works!"

"Yes ..." The professor stroked his beard. "But I don't think I'll proceed with it. Too risky. However, there is *another* invention that you might help me with ..."

Marcus's journey as an apprentice

47

🐾 Ideas for reading 🐾

Written by Gill Matthews
Primary Literacy Consultant

Reading objectives:
- draw inferences such as inferring characters' feelings, thoughts and motives from their actions, and justify inferences with evidence
- predict what might happen from details stated and implied
- identify how language, structure, and presentation contribute to meaning

Spoken language objectives:
- articulate and justify answers, arguments and opinions
- use spoken language to develop understanding through speculating, hypothesising, imagining and exploring ideas
- participate in discussions, presentations, performances, role play, improvisations and debates

Curriculum links: Design and Technology

Interest words: darted, wheeled, swooped

Build a context for reading
- Discuss the front cover of the book. Ask children what they think an apprentice is.
- Read the back-cover blurb. Ask children what they think might happen in the story.
- Discuss what a fantasy story is. Explore children's experience of reading fantasies and what elements they had in common.

Understand and apply reading strategies
- Read pp2–5 aloud. Ask children how they feel about the opening of the story. Discuss how the author has introduced the characters and given an idea of what they are like.
- Read pp6–11 aloud. Discuss how the author has introduced the plot, i.e. Marcus being asked to be the professor's apprentice.
- Ask children how they would describe Marcus and the professor. Support them in making inferences about the characters from their speech, actions and the author's choice of vocabulary.